TEST PREP SANITY
FOR STUDENTS

*What to do, how to think and who to ignore to stay
sane and score high on standardized tests*

by Elie Venezky

Test Prep Sanity for Students:
What to do, how to think and who to ignore to stay sane and
score high on standardized tests
by Elie Venezky

ISBN-13: 978-1987705904
ISBN-10: 1987705904
ISBN DIGITAL: 978-0-615-88458-5
Library of Congress Control Number: 2013916404
Second Edition 2018

Published by Bush Street Press
237 Kearny Street, #174
San Francisco, CA 94108
www.BushStreetPress.com

Book design by Jonathan Burkhardt

Printed in the United States of America

This book would not have been possible without the often blunt opinions of my students. Their help was immeasurable.

This book is dedicated to my mother.

TABLE OF CONTENTS

AUTHOR'S NOTE

Two things you should know before you read this book, and then I'll let you get on with it:

1. Everything I've written has been proven to work over my 20 years of tutoring, even for students who thought I couldn't possibly help them.
2. I'm blunt.

GETTING THE MOST OUT OF THIS BOOK

Why You Should Read This Book

YOU wouldn't go to the gym in dress shoes and a suit. You could, but the workout would be harder and you'd get worse results. And it would suck.

But many of you people (students) are doing the equivalent when you prepare for your standardized tests. You're studying stupidly, which makes you work harder and get worse results. And it sucks.

This book can help you prepare for your exam the right way. It will be very valuable if you read it and apply its advice. You'll learn:

* How to study smartly, so you learn more while studying less
* How to change your attitude about your chances for success
* How to deal with difficult parents so you have more freedom
* Activities and exercises that can improve your score
* How to deal with test anxiety
* Whose exam advice to listen to and whose to ignore

To help you, I've kept this book short. All you have to do is read it. On that note, the really important information is in Chapters 1-8. The technical information, such as explanations of the exams and what they cover, how to register for an exam and where to find the best books for your preparation are all in the Appendix in Chapter 9. If you hate reading, you only have to read the first eight chapters.

A wise man can learn from the biggest fool, but a fool cannot learn from even the wisest of men.

You're Unique and You're Not

Why this Book Can Help You:

When I was younger, I had a bad temper. People often told me that when I felt myself getting angry, I should stop and take three deep breaths. I ignored these people because they didn't understand me, and while their sad little advice may work for morons, I was different. My anger was deep and true and it couldn't be stopped by something as easy as taking three deep breaths.

And then when I was 27, I tried it and it worked.

I'm telling you this story because I've met a lot of students with similar attitudes. They don't think anyone can possibly understand or help them. As a result, they carry around issues for years without ever trying to fix them. They believe that they're unique and therefore can't be helped by general advice.

If this description fits you, know that you're unique because of the combination of your thoughts and experiences, not because each thought and experience itself is unique. We all look different because of the combination of our features, not because no one else has ever had brown hair and small ears. And just because we look different doesn't mean I can't help you get rid of acne.

Similarly, I don't fully understand you, but this book can still help you because maybe I've gone through something similar to you, or I've helped one of my students get past obstacles similar to yours. So don't be a moron like I was and wait until you're in your late twenties to take anyone's advice.

Stupid and Important

How to View Your Test:

Whatever test you're taking, it's stupid. It's judging your intelligence by giving you timed questions that have little to do with your ability to do well in school or in life. Success in real life – you'll be happy to know – has little to do with geometry or vocabulary questions. Therefore, standardized tests are stupid.

Whatever test you're taking, it's important. The people who decide if you get into their schools use it to make their decisions.

If you do well, you'll have a much better shot at getting what you want. Therefore, standardized tests are important.

There you have it. These tests are both stupid and important. If this is the first time you realize that something can be both stupid and important, then today is a very important day for you. Congratulations.

Should Vs. Is

You may be thinking that stupid things shouldn't be important and that tests shouldn't count as much as they do. You're right. Congratulations, again. Now start studying. Don't live in the world of what should be true; live in the world of what is true. And what's definitely true is that your test score matters a lot.

To adapt a quote from Nicolas Cage in *Lord of War*: you may think these tests are evil. But unfortunately for you, they're a necessary evil.

I'm Not a Good Test-Taker!

Why that's Crap:

You may think you're not a good test-taker because you've done poorly on tests in the past. You may be right.

Probably, though, you've just never learned the material the right way and your attitude sucks. You're doing the equivalent of holding a tennis racket by the wrong end, hitting the ball into the net and then complaining that you're just not a good tennis player.

To be clear, I'm not saying you're a great test-taker now; I'm saying that whatever your problem is, it's fixable and you can become a good test-taker.

Students have different ways of learning, and schools cater to exactly one of those ways. Just because you've had trouble with a topic in school doesn't mean you can't learn it.

And even if you were a bad test-taker, which is probably not true, you can still do well on this exam.

Standardized tests aren't magic. They're math, reading, maybe vocabulary and grammar questions. All of these subjects are learnable. So stop thinking of yourself as a bad test-taker; you're just making your life harder.

You're Preparing for a Test, Not Giving Birth.

It Doesn't Have to Hurt.

You may think studying for these exams has to be painful and difficult. It doesn't. You'll have to work hard, but you're not digging trenches in the Sahara desert in August. You're studying for an exam.

If you follow the guidelines in this book, you can make the process much easier. This book has a lot of tips on everything from what to eat to how to learn to how to get your parents off your back.

And not only will the entire process be easier, but you'll do better on your exam.

Why?

I give a lot of advice in this book. Some of it may seem strange, and you may wonder why I want you to follow it. There's only one reason for everything I tell you to do: It will get you the highest possible score with the least possible effort. The reason for that is so you get accepted into as many schools as possible.

Why Should I Listen to You?

You may be wondering who I am and why you should listen to me. I'll tell you.

I've been tutoring students for standardized tests for 20 years, and I've worked with teens for over 25 years. I've helped a lot of students get standardized test scores they never imagined they could achieve, and I've helped a lot of students get into high schools and colleges they never thought they could get into.

I was also a dumb and angry teenager. I thought everyone was full of crap and spent my teens and early twenties bitching about what I didn't like.

It wasn't until my late twenties that I stopped looking for reasons to be angry. So I'm not some guy who's always successful and who's going to tell you to just smile and life will be a non-stop wonderland of unicorns and candy. I'm someone who's been both crushingly pessimistic and reasonably optimistic, and I can tell you without reservation that optimism is better.

So, if you're wondering why you should listen to me, you can choose between the fact that I've helped a ton of people somewhat like you succeed and the fact that I've experienced a lot of things you may be experiencing right now.

It's on You

The advice in this book doesn't work on its own. You have to read and follow instructions. With this book and hard work — and maybe a tutor — you'll have everything you need to do well, but none of that will matter if you don't try.

You may be the kind of person who thinks not trying is better than failing. I had this attitude for a long time, and if you believe nothing else I tell you in this book, believe this: that attitude is crap.

Imagine something you're good at. Now imagine someone who sucks at it coming up and telling you, "I could be good, but I just don't try." How do you feel about that person?

Not trying doesn't excuse a poor test performance; it makes it worse because you were too afraid to try.

If you've never really tried at school and think it's too late to start, then you can benefit from the following Chinese proverb:

The best time to stop being a jerk is 40 years ago. The second best time is right now.

There you go. You can't go back in time, so you're going to have to choose the second best time to start trying.

CHAPTER 2

YOU, THE STUDENT

Your attitude

Do not be discouraged ever, as you struggle along the way. It is the greatest possible detriment to your progress, the worst obstacle you can create to block your path.

-Swami Paramananda

Your attitude matters a lot. In most cases, it matters as much as your materials and your tutor. So...

Stay Positive

The reason you need a positive attitude is not that mystical energy will flow out of your butt and into a magical universe of love and happiness. The reason you need a positive attitude is that people with positive attitudes try harder than people with negative attitudes.

It's as simple as that. If you think you're going to succeed, you'll look at difficulties as temporary problems you can overcome. If you think you're going to fail, you'll see those same difficulties and give up.

And there will be difficulties.

Test-makers purposely make questions difficult to understand so that students give up without trying. But while these questions are difficult to understand, they're not that difficult to answer. You just have to keep working until you understand them. And to keep working, you need to believe your work is going to pay off.

There comes a point in every student's progress when attitude and hard work matter more than intelligence. Again:

There comes a point in every student's progress when attitude and hard work matter more than intelligence.

How Do I Have a Positive Attitude When I'm No Good at Tests?

Fair question. Like I said earlier, I'm not asking you to believe that you're a great test-taker right now: many of you suck, and me claiming otherwise would be a lie. You wouldn't believe me, anyway. When I say you need to have a positive attitude, I mean you need to believe that you can learn what you need to learn.

Believe that you can learn what you need to learn.

If you're taking the SAT and scoring in the 1100s, believe that you can get your score up to 1200. Once you're there, start believing that you can get to 1250. Take it in small steps - only so much that your goal stretches your beliefs without breaking them.

9

I've worked with a lot of students who sucked at standardized tests, and the ones who worked hard and believed they could succeed made huge improvements. You may think sucking at tests is a permanent part of who you are, but it's not.

If you have a negative attitude and have no idea how you can switch to a positive attitude, here are two ridiculous-sounding but scientifically proven ways you can change your attitude:

1. Fake it

Once every morning and once every night say the following phrase: "I'm getting better at this test."

2. Rename it

The reason most students are bad at standardized tests is not some permanent, inner deficiency. It's usually one or more of the following:

* They had a bad teacher and didn't learn some important foundation early on.
* They've never worked hard, or even kind of hard.
* They've never been taught how to take a standardized test.
* They just don't care.

If you think of yourself as a bad test-taker, stop it. From now on, view yourself as a beginning student who's just now learning how to take a test.

If you think these exercises are stupid and can't possibly work, you're half-right. They are unbelievably stupid and they absolutely work. In scientific trials, the act of regularly repeating a belief has shown to make the speaker actually believe it, and renaming an attitude and condition has been shown to increase motivation and success.

You learned earlier that something can be both stupid and important; now you're learning something can be both stupid and effective.

Things can be both stupid and effective.

If you don't believe me, think of all the dumb things that are successful. Look at the stupid movies that everyone sees or the stupid games everyone plays. If you think just because someone or something is stupid, he/she/it can't work effectively, then you're the dumb one.

You still have to study; a positive attitude isn't a magic pill. But you'll have greater success and a better time if you focus on the positive and stay optimistic.

How to Look at the Test

When I was eight years old, I was sure I'd be a horrible driver. I was sure I'd steer right into oncoming traffic and kill myself and everyone else in the car the first time I got behind the wheel. I thought this way because I was eight, very short and sat in the back of my parents' large car. I couldn't see the road properly, so everything seemed random and impossible.

Eventually, I got taller and moved to the front seat. Suddenly, I saw what driving required and it didn't seem that hard.

If you think the test is impossible, it's because, metaphorically, you're eight, short and sitting in the back seat. You don't have a clear view of how you'll do on the test because you're not seeing the test properly.

> *You don't have a clear view of the test, so your view of your own ability is probably wrong.*

As you study and learn, your confidence will grow and the way you view the test will change. Gradually, you'll realize that doing well is not random and impossible but the result of clear and basic steps you can take.

How to View the Work

There's a lot to learn. Don't try to learn it all at once. Any job, no matter how big, can be accomplished by breaking it into smaller steps. You don't eat a big steak by cramming it all in your mouth at once; you take small bites.

The following quote from Empire Falls by Richard Russo sums it up:

> *Mrs. Whiting remained undaunted for the simple reason that she never, ever allowed herself to dwell on the magnitude of whatever task she was confronted with. What she possessed was the marvelous ability to divide the chore into smaller, more manageable tasks. Once this diminishment was accomplished, her will became positively tidal in its persistence.*

If you're terrible at geometry, don't try to learn all of geometry at once. Start with triangles. When you've learned triangles, move on to rectangles and squares.

If you're bad at grammar, learn how to recognize subject-verb disagreement. When you have that down, you can worry about misplaced modifiers.

Focusing on the big picture makes a task look unconquerable. Focus on small steps and you'll improve quickly.

How to View Mistakes

Stupid people think being smart means not making mistakes. Smart people know they'll make mistakes and learn from them. When you're studying, look at your mistakes as gifts. You just learned where you need help during practice, when it doesn't count, as opposed to on the actual exam, when it does. If you still need more convincing, fill out the chart on the following page.

Something I'm Good at
How I Learned

1. Instruction
2. Others' Mistakes
3. Your Own Mistakes

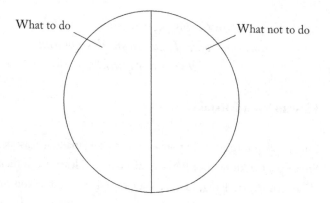

Pick something you're good at doing. It doesn't have to be academic; in fact, it's better if it isn't. It could be a video game or a sport or dancing or almost anything.

Being good at something means knowing what to do and what not to do. There are generally three ways of learning: through instruction, through other's mistakes, and through your own mistakes.

Start with "What to do." What percentage of that did you learn from instruction? Draw a line in that semicircle that shows that percentage.

How much did you learn from watching others' mistakes? Draw a line that marks that percentage.

Tutoring

How I Learned

1. Instruction
2. Others' Mistakes
3. Your Own Mistakes

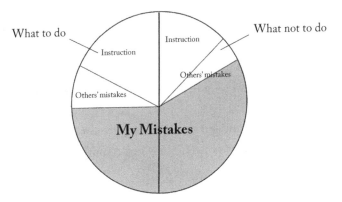

Finally, how much did you learn by making mistakes and correcting yourself? Draw a line and then shade in that part.

Now repeat the process with how you learned what not to do. How much did you learn from instruction? How much from others' mistakes? How much from your own mistakes? Now shade in the part of the circle that shows your own mistakes.

I did one for tutoring. It's shown above. I'm a great tutor, and over half of what I've learned is from making mistakes. Likewise, I contend that you're good at whatever it is you're good at not in spite of your mistakes, but because you learned from them.

Becoming skilled at something doesn't come from being perfect; it comes from learning from your mistakes.

How to Get Motivated

I've heard the following a lot:

"I hate this test and I don't want to study. Why can't I get motivated?"

Why would you feel motivated? You don't like studying; of course you don't want to do it. That's what not liking something means.

That beam of light you're waiting for to fill you with peace, love and the motivation to study isn't coming. Just sit down and start working.

Stop waiting for divine intervention.
Just start studying.

It'll get easier. But if you wait till you really, truly, in your heart of hearts feel like studying, you will die before you crack open a book.

Yeah, But I Can't Get myself to Work

Starting is the hardest part of any process. So start small. If your test has vocabulary, study some vocabulary. If you can stand it, get your parents to help. If your test doesn't have vocabulary, start with the part you like best. If you're good at math, do some practice math problems. If it's reading you like most, start with some reading comprehension.

One of the best things you can do to move past procrastination is to set an end time. Set a timer for 30 minutes. Sit at your desk. It doesn't matter if you get nothing done, stay there. When the timer goes off, you're done. Don't work any more; next time you can set the timer for longer.

How to View Your Progress

People think progress should look like this:

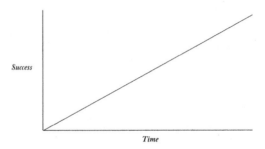

Success

Time

It doesn't always look that way. Sometimes it looks like this:

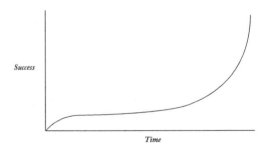

Success

Time

Sometimes you work for a while and it doesn't seem like you're improving. That doesn't mean you aren't. Sometimes improvement takes time to kick in.

Yeah, But I Don't Feel Like I 'm Making Any Progress

There are two possible reasons for this feeling:

1. You're making progress and just don't realize it.
2. You're not making any progress.

You're not the best person to recognize your own progress. In fact, you're the worst, and not just on this test, but on most things. You see yourself every day, so small changes don't register, just like it doesn't register when you grow. You never wake up and think, "I grew last night!" But sometime in the last five years, I'm betting you grew.

The best way to tell if you're improving is to go back to your original mock exam or early work and look at the questions you got wrong. Can you solve them now? If you can, you've improved. If you can't, you fall into the second group.

If you're not improving, there could be many explanations. Be completely honest about the following questions:

* Are you working hard?
* Are you working on what you like, or on where you need help?
* Are you reviewing the material?
* Do you care?

If you're not doing any of the above, start doing it. If you are, but you're not improving, it could be your attitude. You could be acting like a fruit fly in a jar.

If you put fruit flies in a jar with a lid, the flies will try to escape by hitting the bottom of the lid. After a little while, though, they'll stop trying to escape. Even if you take off the lid, the flies won't fly out of the jar, because they assume the lid is still on. They'll stay there until they die.

Many students act like these flies. They failed in the past, so they think they can't succeed on these tests and don't try to work through difficult problems. They assume they can't get better, so they don't.

Don't be like these flies.

> *Push yourself on hard questions.*
> *Believe you can improve.*

Yeah, thanks, but I can't do well on this test.

> Infallible (adj.) – absolutely trustworthy and sure; unable to be wrong

When I was seven, I thought peanut butter turned to poison if not refrigerated. (Thank you, older neighbor.) If you're like every other human being on the planet, you had at least one equally stupid belief. And like I was, you were absolutely certain you were right. Think of an example now.

Got it? Great. You have now proven that your thoughts are not infallible. If you don't think you can succeed on your test, you're as wrong as I was about peanut butter.

You don't have to admit it now. I wouldn't have when I was your age. Think about it, though: it'll make life easier. And just so we're clear, I'm not saying you *will* do well on this test; I'm saying you *can* do well on this test. Surely you can at least admit that.

If you think you can't do well on your test, you're wrong.

Summary

I make this point a lot throughout this book: you can do well on this test.

It doesn't matter how you've done before. It doesn't matter if you've bombed every standardized test you've ever taken. You have the potential to do well if you prepare the right way.

Have an attitude that helps you improve. Be positive. That doesn't mean you have to think you'll get everything right, but believe you can get better. I promise, at the end of the day, you'll be better for it.

* Stay positive.
* Stretch your beliefs gradually. Don't expect instant perfection; instead, focus on your ability to improve.
* Break your work up into small tasks.
* If you're having trouble studying, set an end time and stick to it.
* Love your mistakes. Study them. Learn from them.
* Don't wait for motivation. Just start working. Do what you like best if that gets you in motion.
* It's not always obvious when you're making progress. Check against past tests and homework. Sometimes progress takes time to kick in.
* If it doesn't seem like you're getting any better, investigate why.
* Push through hard questions.
* Stay positive.

CHAPTER 3

OTHER PEOPLE

Who to listen to, who to ignore,
and how to deal with everyone

Your Friends

Your friends are liars; ignore them.

It's not just your friends who lie. It's pretty much everyone, and if you believe them and let them influence how you look at yourself then you're a sucker.

It's probably not personal. It's just that no one likes to admit their weaknesses or mistakes. People who are scared pretend not to be scared; people who feel stupid pretend not to feel stupid; people who lose $500 gambling say they lost $50. It's human nature: who wants to admit they lost $500?

Lies about studying and getting tutored.

We all want to be the super-genius who can solve the world's hardest math problem with just one glance. But you're not that person. I'm not that person, either. Neither are your friends.

So if a friend says, "I didn't study at all and I got a perfect score," they're probably lying. And if they say they're not getting tutored for the exam, they might be lying, too. Many of my students have told me that they lie about not getting tutored.

Anxiety

You'll hear lies and bad advice aplenty in regard to anxiety, in both directions.

Some students are very anxious about the exam and want to make everyone else anxious, too. It's like they've contracted this great new disease and can't wait to share it. Ignore these people. Just because they're anxious doesn't mean you have to be.

Likewise, if someone tells you they're not anxious at all about the exam, they're probably lying. If they're not, ask them how they do it; maybe you can learn from them.

Either way, it doesn't matter, because you're not your friends. However you feel is how you feel. Just admit it and know that it's not wrong.

> *Your friends lie. Ignore them if what they say doesn't work for you.*

Do what works for you

If you need tutoring for a test, get tutoring, just like if you need glasses to see clearly, get glasses. It doesn't matter if your friends have perfect vision. You still need them. Why is studying different?

Your friends may be great people. If so, feel free to listen to their advice. But understand that most people think that what worked for them will work for everyone, and that's not the case: different people need different things.

> **What works for your friends won't necessarily work for you. Don't trust them over your own experience.**

Rumors

You people love spreading rumors about tests. Every year I hear new ones and they're all stupid. Don't waste time worrying about them. If you think a rumor might be true, and it makes you nervous or upset, ask your tutor or guidance counselor. If they don't know, call the people who make the test and ask them. The names and numbers of the test-makers for your exam are in the Appendix of this book.

Older Weird People

Every once in a while when I was younger, an older person would corner me and dispense some really bad advice. It was usually told in a tone of angry desperation or total self-assurance. Maybe there were just a lot of weirdos where I grew up.

Regardless, understand that when most people give you advice, they're talking half to you and half to the younger version of themselves, so their advice might not even fit you.

There's no hard and fast rule for determining who's giving you good advice and who's not, but be suspicious of any extremes and remember that most people believe what worked for them will work for everyone, and that's just not true.

Your Parents

Many students want their parents to leave them alone, then act in ways that ensure that never happens.

The best way to get your parents to leave you alone is to communicate with them and let them know that you're doing your work and that it's going well.

If your first thought on reading the above was "I don't want to talk to my parents!" then you have missed the point. I'm not asking if you want to communicate with your parents; I'm telling you to communicate with your parents, at least if you want more freedom.

You may not know how to communicate with your parents. I go into detail on how in the next chapter. For right now, though, I'm going to explain to you a little about why your parents act the way they do.

First off, imagine you're on a plane and there's a lot of turbulence. Which of the following would you prefer?

* The pilot gets on the loudspeaker and explains what's going on and how it will all be OK.
* The pilot remains silent, even after five minutes of heavy turbulence.

Which of those two makes you more comfortable? Which one has you constantly trying to get the flight attendant's attention?

Communicate with your parents.

Their motives.

Probably, your parents care about you and want you to do well. They may have a weird way of showing it, but deep down they most likely want you to succeed. And for them, the experience of a child taking a standardized test is a lot like sitting on an airplane going through heavy turbulence.

Basically, they're worried. Applying to college or high school is very different now than it was when they were young, so a lot of parents feel lost. To make matters worse, they're probably getting a lot of crap thrown their way from other parents.

When parents are worried, they need more information from you. The less you give them, the more worried they'll be and the more they'll involve themselves in your life. The more you give them, the more relaxed they'll be. Since they can't read your mind, you're going to have to communicate with them.

Yeah, but my parents are annoying.

Ok, maybe, but think about what you want. If it's more free time, then act to calm your parents down. If it's to have a mutually irritating relationship in which your refusal to share any information forces them to constantly ask you what's going on, then by all means continue with the silent treatment.

Tell them the following (adjust slightly to fit your personality):

> Mom, Dad, I know you want me to do well and that you're nervous about the test. I'm nervous, too, and talking about the test only makes me more nervous. So I will give you a 15 minute update every Sunday and Wednesday evening about what's going on and what I need. In return, I need to not talk about it the rest of the time. Does that sound fair?

If they don't think it's fair, ask why.

As a heads-up, this approach won't work if you don't actually study and do your work.

Set up a schedule.

If you let your parents know that you're studying for your standardized test on Mondays and Thursdays from 7:00-8:30, and you do it, your parents will leave you alone a lot more.

They won't have to ask "Are you studying?" because they'll already know.

Set up a schedule. It'll calm your parents down and they'll pester you less.

Let them help you once in a while.

Depending on your relationship with your parents, you can make your life easier by letting them help you study.

If you let your parents help you, they'll see that you're working, so they'll ask you fewer questions. Plus, they can help you get your work done. If your test has vocabulary, let your parents help you study it.

Most students have trouble motivating themselves to study vocabulary, which is too bad, because on some tests - specifically the ISEE and SSAT - it's very important. And for most students, the issue isn't that studying is difficult to do; it's that studying is difficult to start. Parents can help.

Ask your parents to quiz you for 10 minutes, once in the morning and once in the evening, three times a week.

Letting your parents help you study once in a while helps you get work done and gets them off your back. It's a worthwhile price to pay.

I'm not totally clueless. I know some parents are crazy and impossible to work with. If your parents are crazy, you don't have to work with them.

Your Guidance Counselor

Don't get your guidance counselor angry. They're going to write about you on your application, and believe me, there are code words they can use if you're a prick.

If you disagree about something, explain your side rationally. If you think you're ready to take the SAT or ACT and they don't, explain that you've done a lot of studying. If you've taken mock exams (and you should have), show them your scores. Guidance counselors are usually rational. If yours isn't, do your best to avoid upsetting them.

Don't get your guidance counselor angry.

Your Teachers

You're going to need some recommendations from teachers, so try not to be a total jerk to all of them.

Just like with guidance counselors, there are code words that teachers use when writing recommendations that will let colleges know if you're a pain in the ass. And teachers talk to other teachers, so don't think just because you've gotten along well with a couple of teachers you can be a jerk to the rest.

Don't be a total pain in the ass to your teachers.

Again, you don't have to clean erasers after school. But don't go out of your way to be obnoxious.

29

Summary

Other people can be either very helpful or very harmful when you're studying for a standardized test. You can control the effect that other people have on you if you follow the advice in this chapter.

* Ignore rumors or ridiculous claims, or at least ask your tutor, guidance counselor or the test-makers if they're true.
* Don't compare yourself to your friends. Do what works best for you.
* Deal with what you're feeling, not with how you think you should feel.
* Communicate with your parents and you'll have more free time. Let them help you once in a while if you can stand it.
* Set up a study schedule and stick to it.
* Don't get your teachers angry and don't get your guidance counselor angry. If you have a disagreement, present your side calmly.

CHAPTER 4

STAYING SANE

Why it's a good idea and how to do it

The Case for Sanity

You may have a lot going on in your life right now. Studying for this test, if you're anxious and already busy and feeling pressured by people around you, may make you feel like going crazy.

Going crazy may seem like a good idea. Many bad ideas do in the moment. It's not. Stay sane. You may not want to hear it, but the following will help you avoid getting sent upstate to some place that doesn't let you have sharp things.

Be Communicative

When I was eight, my mom stopped buying the brand of ice cream I liked and started buying crappy ice cream. Eight is an age when ice cream matters a lot, so I was legitimately upset. But my mother had no idea, because I never said anything. So the crappy ice cream kept coming, until, finally, the brand went out of business.

The moral of this story is:

People can't read your mind. If you need something, ask for it.

How to Ask

You may be thinking, "I ask for things all the time, and I don't get them!"

The problem could be with the way you're asking and not necessarily with what you want. There's a way to describe what you need that works and a way that doesn't. I've heard a lot of you people ask for things from your parents, and if I were them, I wouldn't have given them to you, either.

Here's the big key:

Don't be such a jerk.

Present what you need in a way that doesn't make them choose between giving you what you want and keeping their pride.

Describe your situation calmly and rationally. If you can't find the right way to explain why you think something is true, but feel deeply that it is, say exactly that: "I'm having trouble finding the right words, but I really feel this is true.

If you have one of those weeks in school when you have a test in every subject, calmly tell your tutor or parents the following:

"Next week is insane for me in school. I have tests in_____ and_____. Could I have less homework this week, please?"

If you're having a really bad day, and you can say, "I'm having a rough day, I need to listen to music and blow off steam for an hour," without yelling or sounding bitchy, then you are much more likely to get what you want.

What if my parents and tutor don't listen?

Then that sucks. But you're right where you would be if you hadn't said anything, and at least you tried.

If your parents don't listen to you, ask them why not. You might not love the answer, but it's a quick way to get the problem out in the open.

Have a Release

Find something that you enjoy doing that calms you down and do it regularly. If you're not sure what that could be, try things: listening to music, lifting weights, screaming into your pillow - who cares as long as it works?

Notice When You're Getting Upset

Most people notice they're losing their temper only after the point of no return.

If you feel yourself starting to get a little crazy, do something about it right then. Take a 15-minute break and move around.

The old adage, "An ounce of prevention is worth a pound of cure," is especially true as far as craziness is concerned.

Find a way to blow off steam and do it when you start to feel crazy, not after you lose your temper.

Schedule Wisely

Don't be a moron. If you save all your weekend homework for Sunday night, don't schedule a tutoring session for Sunday night or Monday evening; you don't need the extra work.

If you play a sport that has regularly scheduled games, work around them.

If your test is coming up in two months, and your schedule is jam-packed with extra activities until then, think about cutting some of them out for a couple of months. I know you may want to do everything, but sometimes trying to do everything just means you do nothing well.

Recognize and Admit Your Emotions

Many people feel at the mercy of their emotions, which they believe just happen to them. But we're actually creating our emotions constantly. Wyatt Woodsmall, Ph.D, a leading expert on retraining thinking patterns, talks about three key methods we use to create our emotions:

* The images we play in our heads
* The words we say to ourselves
* The tonality of our inner voices

Most students (and adults, for the record) aren't very nice to themselves. In fact, we talk to ourselves in ways we would never talk to anyone else or allow ourselves to be talked to by others.

We berate ourselves; we call ourselves stupid; we are sarcastic and mocking of our efforts. And then we wonder why we're upset. If you want to better control your emotions, pay careful attention to the three methods listed above and treat yourself as you would treat someone you love and support.

If you make a big mistake, admit it, but don't sit around calling yourself stupid. Realize what you did and take steps to make sure you don't do it again.

Admit your mistakes without beating yourself up.

How to Deal With Emotions

Once an emotion hits you, admit it. An emotion is like someone screaming your name and trying to get your attention. If you ignore them, they're only going to scream louder.

If you're upset, feel upset. You don't have to scream or cry if you don't want to. Just admit it. And don't feel like you have to be happy all the time; that's impossible. It's fine to be pissed off every once in a while.

Admit what you're feeling.

If you want to lessen a negative emotion, explain out loud what you're feeling in your body. It sounds dumb, but we already talked about how dumb things can be effective.

Here's an example:

> I'm feeling a lot of energy in my chest. I feel jittery in my legs, and it's difficult to sit still. My chest is warm and the muscles in my face are tight.

Why Explaining Helps

The amygdala is the part of your brain responsible for many negative and base human emotions, such as fear and anger. When you're triggered, you send activity to the amygdala, which makes you angry or scared or whatever the appropriate response is.

Your prefrontal cortex is responsible for higher functions, such as the ability to describe feelings. When you're describing something, you send activity to your prefrontal cortex.

Therefore, when you start describing your negative state and how it feels, you're taking activity away from your amygdala and moving it to your prefrontal cortex, which lessens the severity of your negative state.

If You Have Severe Test Anxiety, Get Help

Just about everyone gets nervous about standardized tests. It's normal, and anxiety can actually be helpful if you use it the right way (more on this, later). But extreme test anxiety, where you can't breathe and everything looks different and you can barely hold it together, needs outside help.

In the Test Prep section, I talk in detail about how to deal with test anxiety. If you think you have severe test anxiety, do something about it now, because severe anxiety affects your studying, not just your test-taking.

Summary

Staying sane is much better than going crazy. Trust me. The best ways to stay sane are as follows:

* Pay attention to your emotions and do something before you lose control.
* Admit what you're feeling and don't feel guilty if you feel bad.
* Have a release, such as working out or listening to music.
* Treat yourself well. Make sure your inner dialogue is supportive.
* Communicate what you need calmly and rationally. People don't always see things the same way you see them, so make sure you explain what you need and how having it will help.
* Schedule your time wisely so you're not overburdened.
* Don't be a jerk.

CHAPTER 5

THE TESTS

The what, the why and the how

Why and How They Cause Such Trouble

You may be an "A" student, but if you haven't studied specifically for your standardized test, you might not be prepared. Don't learn the hard way that good grades don't always mean high test scores.

Standardized tests are harder than school exams. Standardized tests cover a wider array of topics and they cover them in different ways than school exams do. Basically, you're playing a different game. You've been playing slow-pitch softball and now you have to play fast-pitch baseball. Your skills won't necessarily translate.

Why Standardized Tests Are Different

The purpose of school exams is to measure what students know. The purpose of standardized tests is to separate students along a bell curve so schools can decide more easily who they let in and who they don't.

To achieve this bell curve, standardized tests must separate the good students from the great and the great from the truly exceptional. Most use tricky questions and new question types because most students aren't prepared for tricky or new questions.

It's not your fault. Test-makers exploit the way material is taught and tested in school. The following is an example:

> *A circle and a triangle are on a coordinate plane. Which of the following could be the total number of points of intersection of the two objects?*
>
> $$I.\ 2$$
> $$II.\ 5$$
> $$III.\ 6$$
>
> *(A) None*
> *(B) I only*
> *(C) III only*
> *(D) I and III only*
> *(E) I, II and III*

Many students will skip this problem without trying it because they think there's a formula or some specific information they need but don't know. But there's no formula for this question: you just have to start drawing triangles and circles and see if you can get them to intersect in 2, 5 and 6 places. The answer is (E), for the record.

Standardized tests trick students into skipping questions they could answer.

I totally would have gotten that on a test!

Maybe so, friend, and maybe not. It's one thing to look at a question now, with no pressure or time restraints, and say it's easy. It's another thing on the actual test, with a time limit and a sense of urgency.

This problem shows what I mean when I say that attitude can mean more than intelligence on standardized tests. Students who believe in themselves will try things out because they think they can find the answer. Students who don't believe in themselves don't try because why bother?

So yes, you totally can get questions like the one above when you take the test, but you have to stick with them, and that takes confidence.

How Standardized Tests Are Different from School Exams

Math

Math education in most schools goes as follows: you learn a subject, such as percent, and then you're tested on percents. You're only given problems you've seen before. Then the class moves on to ratio and ratio is tested using only problems covered in class. Then the class moves on to exponents and the cycle continues.

This method is terrible for the following reasons, all of which lead to lower test scores:

* It gives a narrow, disconnected view of math in which there's no relation between different subjects (such as percent and ratio).
* It doesn't teach problem recognition or application skills.
* It results in students giving up on questions they could answer.

Let's look at these reasons in more detail:

It gives a narrow, disconnected view of math in which there's no relation between different subjects.
Students who truly understand math and see how it all fits together better understand questions and how to solve them. They know there are only a certain number of ways to solve problems, so they're better at approaching unfamiliar problems and are quicker at finding shortcuts.

Students who don't understand how the subjects fit together have a much harder time solving problems because every solution seems random and the methods for solving problems seem limitless. They have trouble finding shortcuts and understanding new problems.

The difference between the two types of students is the difference between seeing a maze from a bird's eye view and seeing a maze from the inside. In other words, the first type of student can see the big picture. Students who see the big picture don't get lost, because they know where they are and where they need to get to.

It doesn't teach problem recognition or application skills.

What are application skills?
Application skills are the ability to apply your knowledge to questions you haven't seen before. For instance, you may know that perpendicular lines have slopes with a product of -1. The exam may test your ability to apply this knowledge by asking you for the product of the slopes of the four sides of a square in which no sides are perpendicular to either axis.

If you're in high school and the previous question makes no sense, then you, my friend, need to study for the math section of your exam.

A lack of application skills is extremely detrimental on a standardized test, because so many questions are different from what students see in school. This difference is not accidental; it's how test-makers separate students.

A lack of recognition skills, the ability to recognize what type of problem you're facing, is equally detrimental because standardized tests disguise their math questions. School exams generally don't do this, so students never build the necessary skills and end up skipping questions they know how to solve because they don't recognize them.

It results in students giving up on questions they could answer. Giving up is the silent killer of standardized test scores. Since school math exams only have familiar questions, students develop the following mindset: if it doesn't make sense the first time I read it, I don't know how to do it.

Standardized tests contain a lot of math problems that are difficult to understand but easy to solve. When students give up after only reading a question once, they throw away points. The enemy of success on standardized tests isn't making mistakes; it's not trying.

This fact is why confidence is so important. Confident students reread confusing questions; insecure students skip them. Too many students give up on math questions too quickly, and it's because they don't have to fight through difficult, new questions in school. The following is an example of an SAT problem that most students skip, even though many of them know everything they need to solve it:

A right triangle has an area of 30. If one side is 5, what is the perimeter of the triangle?

(A) 12
(B) 13
(C) 25
(D) 30

Below is what you need to solve this problem:

The Pythagorean Theorem: $a^2 + b^2 = c^2$

The formula for the area of a triangle: $\dfrac{base \; x \; height}{2}$

The knowledge that the two legs of a right triangle serve as the base and height

If you've studied geometry in the last two years or prepped at all for your exam, you should know the above formulas and the last fact.

To solve this problem, first draw the triangle:

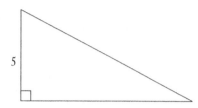

In a right triangle, the two smaller sides serve as the base and height, so you can plug what you know into the formula for area:

$$\frac{base \; x \; height}{2} = area$$

$$\frac{base \; x \; 5}{2} = 30$$

$$base = 12$$

Since the two legs of the right triangle are 5 and 12, you can use the Pythagorean Theorem to find the length of the hypotenuse:

$$a^2 + b^2 = c^2$$
$$5^2 + 12^2 = c^2$$
$$169 = c^2$$
$$13 = c$$

The sides are 5, 12 and 13, so the perimeter of the triangle is 30.

I've given this problem to a lot of students, and I can tell who's going to get it right by whether the student draws the triangle. The ones who draw the triangle work their way through the problem.

But here's the thing: to draw the triangle, to even try to do this problem, you have to believe there's some chance you can get it right. A lot of students don't think they have a chance, so they just move on. Again, why bother if you don't think you can succeed?

In this way, believing you're going to fail becomes a self-fulfilling prophecy: a student thinks they're going to fail, so they don't do the work needed to get the question right. They fail, not because of destiny or stupidity, but because their negative attitude got in the way of trying to solve the problem.

Reading

Most English classes have you reading books, not short passages. Then you write essays; you don't answer multiple-choice questions designed to trick you. You're out of practice for these questions.

In addition, many of you people don't read actively, and standardized test questions take advantage of that fact by having questions that:

* Are partially but not fully correct.
* Are true, but don't answer the question asked. An example of this point follows:

> *Mary loved Jim, but she could not accept his proposal of marriage. There were just too many doubts. Jim had trouble keeping a job, and he lacked ambition. What really killed the marriage, however, was that Jim had been unfaithful. She could not commit to a man who had cheated on her.*
>
> *Why did Mary refuse Jim's marriage proposal?*
>
> *(A) He could not hold down a job.*
> *(B) He had no ambition.*
> *(C) He was a jerk.*
> *(D) He was unfaithful.*

While (A), (B) and arguably (C) are true, only (D) is correct. Not being an active reader will hurt a little if you're reading a 300-page book that you're discussing regularly in class. It will hurt a lot, however, if you're reading a five-paragraph passage with tricky questions at the end.

> *Be an active reader. There is no greater skill for the reading section of your test.*

How do I do that?

Practice. Pay attention to what you're reading instead of letting the words wash over you. If you don't understand a specific part of the text, read it again. If you don't know a word, try to figure out what it means by the words around it. Ask yourself questions as you read, such as "what is the author's main point?" and "how does this part fit into that main point?" It may be tough at the beginning if you've never done it before, but it's worth it.

Grammar

Most students study grammar by learning the rules. Rarely, if ever, do they study how these rules are broken. Then they take a test where they have to spot grammatical errors on questions designed to trick them. Why would we expect them to do well?

> *Directions: After reading each passage, choose the answer to each question that most effectively improves the quality of writing in the passage or that makes the passage conform to the conventions of standard written English.*

> *Many specialists argue that the amount of homework given to high school students prevent the growth of creativity and social skills.*

> *(A) NO CHANGE*
> *(B) prevent the growth for*
> *(C) prevents the growth of*
> *(D) prevents the growth for*

Most students choose answer choice (A), NO CHANGE, which is incorrect. The subject of the sentence is "amount," which is singular, so the verb should be "prevents," answer choice (C).

Because the prepositional phrase "to high school students" comes between the subject and the verb, the sentence doesn't sound incorrect when read quickly, and most students solve these problems by reading them once, quickly.

You must actively look for errors on grammar questions.

Essays

To write an essay in under an hour, you need to think of ideas and organize your thoughts quickly. Most students aren't good at either of these skills.

On a regular essay you can organize and course-correct as you go. But you just don't have the time on a standardized test, so students who don't write outlines or aren't great at keeping their thoughts organized (which is most of you) struggle on the essay section.

Also, writing an essay in under an hour takes practice, and few students practice.

Practice writing A LOT of essays.

I'm Studying! Why Aren't I Improving?

You might be studying the wrong way. Most students study for their standardized tests the same way they study for school exams. They do math problems they already understand; they read passively; and they write essays without making outlines.

They're just reinforcing bad habits. Why would they improve?

> *If you want to improve, you have to study specifically for your standardized test. You cannot study the same way you do for school.*

So what do I do?

You'll find out in three pages.

Registration

If you live in a large city, especially New York City, register as soon as you know your test date because slots fill up quickly.

A list of websites and phone numbers for registering appears in the Appendix.

The Tests

You'll find information about your test, such as what's on it and how long it is, in the Appendix. There's also a page about whether you should take the SAT or the ACT.

Summary

Standardized tests have a completely different way of testing knowledge than school exams do. You must study specifically for your standardized test. Otherwise, you'll be wasting a lot of time and missing what you most need to learn.

* Study actively. Pay attention to what you're missing and why.
* Read actively. Make sure you understand what's going on.
* Practice a lot.
* Register early for your exam.

CHAPTER 6

TEST PREP

There are smart ways and there are stupid ways to study.
I recommend the smart ways.

Ten Ways to Get the Most out of Studying

Most students go about studying for their standardized tests the same way they study for school exams. In the last chapter, we covered why that's a bad idea: you'll work harder and do worse. What follows are 10 ways to get the most out of your studying, which means you'll get higher scores from less work.

* Believe you can succeed.
* Study actively.
* Pulse your studying.
* Be honest about your weaknesses and work on them.

* Learn from your mistakes.
* Review often.
* Practice as you will play.
* Take mock exams.
* Mark your progress.
* Study often.

Believe you can succeed.

You may be tired of hearing this advice by now, but I don't care. It's important and too many students ignore it. So I'm going to say it again:

> *You must believe you can succeed if you want to fulfill your potential on this exam. The reason is students who believe they will succeed will work through difficulty.*

It's not mystical. I'm not asking you to believe in dragons. I just need you to understand that your belief in how you're going to do will greatly affect how you actually do.

Study actively.

When I was in high school, I had to write a book report on *Heart of Darkness* by Joseph Conrad. I read it, then got the CliffsNotes to help.

Reading the CliffsNotes, I realized what a horrible reader I was: I had missed not only the main themes and motifs, but whole scenes. I wasn't so much reading as looking at words and turning pages. I was a passive reader. I didn't absorb anything I read; all I did was waste my time.

A lot of students study the same way. They read or listen passively and whatever lesson they're supposed to be learning just flies right on by, and all their work is just a waste of time.

Concentrate on what you're studying. If you realize you've gotten to the end of a page and haven't been paying attention to any of it (which happens to everyone, for the record), reread it. If you can't concentrate, take a break.

If you study passively, you're just wasting your time. Study actively.

Pulse your studying.

> *A Swedish lumberjack competition came down to a six-hour log-sawing contest. After three days of competing, the two finalists, Olaf and Sven, were tied. Olaf was young, enormous and could work nonstop. Sven was older with more experience.*
>
> *The bell sounded and both Olaf and Sven started sawing. Olaf worked tirelessly, sawing without a break. Sven, on the other hand, stopped every 45 minutes and went behind a shed for 15 minutes.*
>
> *Olaf built a huge lead, but around the three-hour mark, Sven started gaining on Olaf. Olaf was still sawing at his furious rate, and Sven was still taking breaks behind the shed, but Sven was catching up.*
>
> *At five hours, Sven passed Olaf and went on to win easily. Afterwards, Olaf approached Sven and congratulated him. "But how did you do it?" he asked. "I worked without stopping, and I'm bigger and stronger than you are." Olaf*

paused to think for a moment, then asked, "and what were
you doing behind the shed?"

    Sven looked at him and said, "I was sharpening my
saw."

Concentrating for long periods of time is difficult, and your efficiency will suffer.

The longer you work without a break,
the less effectively you work.

Take breaks. Work for 45 minutes, then take a 15-minute break and do something to reload: move around, listen to music, talk to a friend. Then work for another 45 minutes and take another 15-minute break. Most people get more accomplished in this hour and a half of work than they would if they worked straight through for two hours.

If you have trouble concentrating for 45 minutes, start by studying for as long as you can concentrate. Maybe you study for 15 minutes and take a five-minute break. It doesn't matter at first; you can build stamina as you go.

Be honest about your weaknesses, and work on them.

You might think, "Duh," but many students don't actually study what they need to study.

People in general and students specifically don't like doing things they're bad at (again, duh). So most students, if they're good at math and bad at reading comprehension, study math first and then if there's time do a little reading comp.

I did it when I was in high school. I spent almost all my time studying SAT math, even though I was awesome at math and so-so at reading comp. As a result, I crushed the math section and did so-so on the reading.

Be absolutely honest about where you are. Study where you need help. Spend time on the questions you got wrong. Work on your weaknesses. It may not be fun, but it's not supposed to be fun: it's a test, not summer camp.

Learn from your mistakes.

This point is another one that bears repeating. Standardized tests repeat types of questions often. There are only so many ways to test if someone knows the area of a circle or can recognize subject-verb disagreement. If you see something once, there's a good chance you'll see it again.

Mistakes tell you exactly what you need to work on. Pay attention to them.

Learn why you got something wrong and see what tricked you or what you didn't know how to handle. It's one of the best ways to improve.

Review often.

What good is learning something if you just forget it before your exam? It's like you never learned it. If your test has vocabulary, make sure you keep up to date on the words you learned a month ago. Make sure you remember the math and the key concepts of reading comprehension.

There's no point in learning something if you're just going to forget it before the exam. Review early and often.

> *If you want to forget everything after your exam, fine. Do it then. But not before.*

Practice as you will play.

Many students do practice problems half-assed: they do half a reading comprehension passage and then stop for a break. Or they don't write down work on a math problem. Or they do half a problem and then check the answer to see if they're on the right track.

This half-assing slows your progress. Do practice problems the way you're going to do problems on the actual exam. Work through difficulty; cross out obviously wrong answers; re-read sections of a passage. Establish a habit of fighting through difficulty now so on test day it comes naturally.

Take mock exams.

You have no idea whether you're prepared for your test or not without a mock exam. And don't tell me that you're prepared because you're getting everything right in practice. It's one thing to do problems at your leisure in the comfort of your own home. It's a whole other thing to do timed sections in a classroom surrounded by a bunch of strangers.

Mock exams are essential. They improve stamina; they show you where you're strong and where you're weak; they help you deal with anxiety, and they show you whether you're making progress. Taking a mock exam is the best thing you can do to improve.

You should take at least two mock exams, more if you're dealing with test anxiety.

It's not the same at home.

Take mock exams. If you don't, you're a moron.

Mark your progress.

Studying for a test can be a drag, especially if you don't think you're improving. As I said before, you're the worst person to judge your progress. Make sure you go back and check the problems that gave you trouble early in your prep.

See whether you're improving or not. If you are, it'll give you a boost and you'll feel good. If you're not improving, it's better to know now.

Seeing how you've improved will make studying easier.

Study often.

I've seen this pattern a ton: I tutor a student on Wednesday night. We work for an hour and a half; they learn something and then I give them homework for the next Wednesday. They do nothing for six days, then start their homework late Tuesday night or Wednesday afternoon between school and our session.

In the meantime, they've forgotten what they learned. Now they have to either relearn it or give me some weak excuse about why they couldn't do it.

Do your homework soon after you meet with your tutor. Don't wait a week to start.

You know you've got homework to do. Do it quickly and get it out of the way. Be smart about it: study in small chunks. Your brain learns better that way.

Study often and in short blocks, and you'll learn more quickly and easily.

You're more likely to remember something if you study it three different times for 20 minutes a pop than if you study it once for an hour.

It's how the brain works: short, recurring viewings work better than one long one.

It's better to study vocabulary for 15 minutes, four times a week than once a week for an hour. It's easier to remember how to solve probability questions if you do some of your homework within two days after your tutoring session and some later in the week.

Follow these 10 steps, and you will learn more quickly and easily and do better on your standardized test.

The Intangibles

There are other factors that will make studying for the test easier or harder. They are:

* Sleep
* Diet
* Exercise
* Posture
* Breathing

Get enough sleep.

Many of you people don't get enough sleep. I know you have a lot to do, but you're not doing yourself any favors by not sleeping enough. Not getting enough sleep destroys your ability to understand and remember what you study. Below is a quote from John Medina's *Brain Rules: 12 Principles for Surviving and Thriving at Work, Home and School:*

> *The bottom line is that sleep loss means mind loss. Sleep loss cripples thinking, in just about every way you can measure thinking. Sleep loss hurts attention, executive function, immediate memory, working memory, mood, quantitative skills, logical reasoning ability, [and] general math knowledge.*

As you may have noticed, many of the skills Medina lists are tested directly on just about every standardized test. So get some sleep; your score will improve.

If you have trouble sleeping, meditate before bed. Don't roll your eyes: it works. Many sleep issues are caused by an inability to turn off your brain. Meditation helps do just that. Meditation instructions can be found in the Exercises section of the Appendix.

If meditation isn't helping, I recommend Yogi Bedtime Tea. (Yogi is the brand name, Bedtime Tea is the type.) It contains valerian root, which is good for sleep. You can also purchase straight valerian root or melatonin, another natural sleep aid. I'm not a medical professional, so talk to your doctor if you're taking any medication, as some medications react poorly to certain herbs.

Thanks, tutor-guy, but I have too much work to do and not enough time to do it.

Honestly? I've had students who had no time, and I've also had students who wasted all their time until midnight, then started working.

So which group are you in? Are you constantly checking apps and chatting with friends? Are you taking breaks every five minutes to watch a video on your computer? If you are, you're in the second group. If you're busting your ass and totally focused on one thing at a time and still can't get it all done, you're in the first group.

If you're in the first group, my sympathies are with you. Schedule your time very specifically, if you haven't already. Know that the studying you do between 2:00 and 3:00am is probably not doing you much good. My advice is to pick your least favorite non-mandatory activity and drop it.

If you're in the second group, stop dividing your attention. Don't multitask because your brain can't actually multitask. When you do two things at once, your brain has to shift its attention back and forth, and that tires it out. Everything takes much longer than it should and you don't get as much done.

Focus on one task at a time.
You'll get your work done faster.

Eat well.

The following is a true story:

> *It was two nights before his exam, and Jake was a disaster. He made careless error after careless error. He kept forgetting what questions I had assigned him, even though they were circled on the page in front of him. "Four?! Do I do four next?!!" He could not sit still, and his voice was strained and too loud. Something was really wrong.*
>
> *"Oh no," I thought, "This kid's on drugs!" I would have to tell his parents, and the "I think your kid's on drugs" conversation is a real drag.*
>
> *Then I looked at his dinner, uneaten beside him, and at the empty package of cookies he had just devoured. "Jake, tell me everything you've eaten today."*
>
> *"I had donuts for breakfast. Then at lunch I had a soda and one those little pies. Then after school I had another soda and a candy bar, and now these cookies."*
>
> *Jake was overdosing on sugar, and it had turned him into a total moron.*

Diet affects more than just your physical body; it affects your mental ability, as well. If you load up on sugar, your ability to concentrate will suffer, your ability to retain information will suffer and your test score will suffer.

If you eat sugar all day long, you're going to end up stupid.

You don't have to eat only seaweed and brown rice to get the most out of your brain, but you need a balanced diet, which means vegetables along with meat and carbs. It will make learning easier and increase your test score.

Diet includes drinking enough water, too. The rule that you must drink eight glasses a day is a myth, but you still need to drink water during the day; it'll help you think better.

Exercise.

If you missed it earlier, every time I've met a neuroscientist, I've asked them the best way to wake up the brain. They've all said exercise.

Before you study, do something to get your body moving. Jump rope for two minutes or do 20 jumping jacks or 20 push-ups or 20 sit-ups. When you're pulsing your studying, exercising during your breaks really helps.

Posture.

Here's a test: slouch your shoulders and back and hang your head so you look like a vulture. Now say these phrases:

"I feel great!"

Then say:

"I feel terrible."

Change your body position so you're sitting upright with your shoulders back and your head up.

Say: "I feel great."

Then say: "I feel terrible."

It probably felt more natural to say you felt terrible when you were slouched, and it probably felt more natural to say you felt great when you were sitting upright.

It's not a coincidence. Body posture and physiology affect your mood. It's not only that depressed people slouch and happy people sit with straight backs; slouching can keep you in a depressed state and sitting upright can make you feel better.

Breathing.

As goes your breath, so goes your mood. Notice how your breathing is different when you're anxious or upset than it is when you're calm. I've also noticed personally that holding my breath interferes with my thinking, and many of my students have admitted the same is true for them.

If you find yourself starting to freak out on a test, make sure you're breathing. Most of the time you're not, and that's what's making you freak out.

Dealing With Test Anxiety

Test anxiety is both common and misunderstood. Basic test anxiety makes you feel nervous about a test. The following advice is very helpful in dealing with this type of anxiety:

* Know the test
* Practice a lot
* Eat well
* Sleep well
* Stay positive

Admittedly, it's tough to stay positive when you feel anxious. But positivity can be learned if you work at it. At the very least, stop with the self-defeating thoughts and statements.

Then there's the more serious form of test anxiety, which makes students feel paralyzed and prevents them from thinking clearly when taking or even thinking about taking the test. Symptoms can range from an inability to sit still to vomiting. This type of test anxiety is real and demands attention.

How does test anxiety work?

Test anxiety works like a phobia. It can affect students not just on test day, but throughout the entire test prep process. So it's important to deal with it right away.

Test anxiety puts the student into a state of fight or flight. A body in fight or flight is concerned solely with survival and shuts down all unnecessary functions. Unfortunately, doing well on a written exam that deals with math, reading and grammar is not thought of as necessary to survival.

How do I deal with test anxiety?

First, reframe it. Most people think that test anxiety, or anxiety in general, means they're not supposed to be good at something.

It doesn't. In her book about performance anxiety, *Choke*, Sian Beilock describes the counterintuitive results of a study on stress levels and performance.

When stressed, your body releases the hormone cortisol. To measure someone's level of stress, measure the cortisol level in their saliva. You would assume that the cortisol levels of people who thrive in pressure situations would be much lower than the cortisol levels of people who choke. Surprisingly, this assumption isn't true. People who thrive in high-pressure situations show the same levels of cortisol as people who choke. The only difference was that the thrivers looked at their anxiety as energy, and they used it to excel.

Test anxiety doesn't mean you're not meant to succeed; it actually proves that you have what it takes to dominate your exam. You just have to change your interpretation of what your anxiety means.

That's great. How do I do that?

The advice for dealing with test anxiety that you'll find on the internet is only useful for mild test anxiety. Here it is again:

* Know the test
* Practice a lot
* Eat well
* Sleep well
* Stay positive

All of this advice is important for doing well on the exam, and all of it is worthless as far as dealing with serious test anxiety.

Again, serious test anxiety is a phobia, and you can't deal with a phobia by telling someone to stay positive. "Hey, I know you're terrified of spiders, and there's a big spider on your leg, but you ate well so it should be ok. Just stay positive."

Phobias aren't rational, so you're not going to beat them with rational explanations. You need to attack them where they live: in the unconscious mind. To do that, I recommend NLP or hypnosis.

Hypnosis?! Won't I end up clucking like a chicken?

Calm down. I'm not talking about stage hypnosis where a creepy guy in a tuxedo waves a watch back and forth and you end up thinking you're a prima ballerina. I'm talking about using relaxation methods to change habits.

There may be some people who can get others to think that they're chickens, but I doubt it. Here are some facts about hypnosis that might dispel your misconceptions:

* You will remain conscious at all times during hypnosis.
* You will not do anything you don't want to do.
* There is no such thing as installing a kill word, which when spoken makes you commit horrible acts in service of your new master.

Hypnosis helped me get over my insomnia, which was so bad that I was literally going crazy (and I know what literally means). It worked so well that I got certified as a hypnotist myself, and I've used what I learned to help a lot of students. If I had the power to make them do what I wanted, I would currently have an army of teenagers cleaning my apartment and running my errands.

What's NLP?

Neuro-Linguistic Programming refers to the connections between language, neurological processes and behavioral patterns. We make these connections through our experiences, and we can reorganize them to achieve specific goals in life.

What?!?

Basically, we all have triggers from our past that determine how we respond to specific situations. You may have been scared by a clown when you were young. Now, whenever you see a clown, your thoughts travel a well-worn path that leads to terror. That pathway is not helpful: it's probably embarrassing. NLP can help change that pathway so it leads to a more helpful emotion, such as patience.

Many kids have test anxiety because they did poorly on a standardized test in the past and then decided that they were bad test-takers. That experience led them to fear standardized tests, which led them to tense up during tests, which made them do poorly on tests, which reaffirmed and strengthened their belief that they were bad test-takers. And the cycle continued, creating a self-limiting belief that may no longer be true, but that rational arguments can't shake. NLP can help change that self-limiting belief.

That sounds like crap.

It does. But I've seen NLP and hypnosis work, both on my students and on me. And if I had serious test anxiety, I'd worry less about whether something sounds like crap and more about whether it works.

What else can help with test anxiety?

Take a lot of mock exams.
Mock exams and timed exercises provide small amounts of stress, which help prepare you for larger amounts of stress later on. If you want to jump off the high dive, but you're scared of heights, jump off some lower platforms first to slowly get used to the feeling. Mock exams are like the lower platforms. They get you used to answering questions under the pressure of being timed, scored and evaluated. They make a big difference.

Reframe and rename.
Stop saying you're bad at standardized tests. Your problem is that you've never been taught the right way to take a standardized test. Basically, you're a beginning test-taker. Beginners aren't supposed to get everything right.

But you're working on it and getting better (just by reading this book). So soon you won't be a beginner.

You can beat test anxiety, but you must approach it correctly.

Summary

The way you study will determine how much you learn and, ultimately, how you do on your standardized test. Here are the best ways to study:

* Study actively.
* When you're studying, just study. Don't check email or constantly chat with friends.
* Believe you can succeed.
* Pulse your studying. Take breaks when you need to reload.
* Be honest about your weaknesses and work on them.
* Learn from your mistakes.
* Review often.
* Take mock exams.
* Mark your progress.
* Study often.
* Eat well.
* Sleep enough.
* Watch your posture.
* Breathe.
* Deal with test anxiety if you have it.

CHAPTER 7

TEST DAY

What to do and why, from a month
before to right afterward

The Month Before

A lot of you people have heavy workloads and have pushed your standardized test prep to the sidelines, rushing through your work or changing your study schedule when something more immediate came up. With a month to go before the exam, your test takes priority. If that means missing a music lesson or sports practice for a mock exam, so be it.

Take two mock exams during the final month. Stamina plays a big part in doing well, so get in shape.

Start reviewing problem areas. Go back over any subjects that gave you trouble in the past. Make sure you're ready for every part of the exam.

Two Weeks Before

You may freak out a couple of weeks before the exam. You might feel like you don't know anything; you might feel like you hate the exam and don't want to take it. It's all normal. Accept that you feel crappy, get it out of your system and move on. Know that your thoughts are just an expression of nerves and aren't always accurate.

What to do

* Review any area that you found/still find difficult. If that means writing a bunch of 50-minute essays, write a bunch of essays.
* Go back over your work and look at all the questions you missed.
* Go over test strategy with your tutor, if you have one.
* Schedule time for things you enjoy.

My Parents Are Driving Me Crazy. What Can I Do?

> Mom, Dad, I'm nervous about the test. I'm going to study a lot, but when I'm not studying I need a break from thinking about the exam so I can keep myself from getting too stressed. Here are the times when I'll study. You can check in on me to make sure I'm keeping my word. The rest of the time, I need to not think or talk about the test.

If your parents don't agree, show them the following:

Hi, I'm Elie Venezky. I've been helping students succeed on standardized tests for 20 years. My former tutoring company was voted one of the top 20 tutoring companies for math in New York City, out of over 2,000 companies assessed. I know what I'm talking about. Your child is probably nervous right now, and you may be nervous, too. This close to the exam, your child needs time when they're not thinking about or talking about the exam. If they're studying, let them be and don't talk about the test. Trust me. They'll do better. If they're not studying, take away their phone and lecture them all you want.

The Night Before

The night before the exam you should have everything you need for your exam in a bag ready to go. This includes:

* Admission ticket
* All necessary identification
* At least four sharpened no. 2 pencils
* A watch
* A calculator with extra batteries (if calculators are allowed)
* A bottle of water
* Two snacks, each containing glucose*

    *Complex thinking depletes glucose levels. Don't eat candy bars or pure sugar, but take something to restore your glucose levels, such as oranges, blueberries or strawberries, trail mix, peanut butter and honey sandwiches or cereal.

Getting to the test center

If you're not taking the test at your school, make sure you know how to get to the test center. Plan to get there 15 minutes early.

Should I study?

Conventional wisdom says no; you should do something relaxing, such as watching a movie. I agree with conventional wisdom for most students. But there are some students who won't feel relaxed unless they study. If you're this type, study a little, but stop at least an hour before you go to bed.

Should I go to bed early?

If you get enough sleep, go to bed at your normal time. Only if you're sleep-deprived and can fall asleep early should you go to bed early. If you're just going to toss and turn for an hour, don't bother. Go to bed at your normal time.

The Morning Of

Test day is finally here!

Eat your normal breakfast.

Test day is no time for something new. Eat your normal breakfast, unless your normal breakfast is nothing or pure sugar, in which case eat a light breakfast that's not just cereal made from sugar. Stick to what you know. Now is not the time to start drinking coffee, nor is it the time to stop drinking coffee.

Prepare for bad weather.

Different test centers have different ideas of what a comfortable temperature means. Wear layers and bring an extra sweatshirt.

Exercise.

I've asked a lot of neuroscientists the best way to wake up the brain. They all said "exercise," so do some light exercise, such as jumping jacks or pushups. You don't have to run a half-marathon, but do something to wake up your body and mind.

Bring a lucky charm.

Why not?

During the Test

Speak up.

If your desk is wobbly or you're staring directly into the sun, say something. If it bothers you a little at the beginning of the exam, it's going to bother you a lot two hours in.

Don't talk about the test during your breaks.

Breaks are your time away from the exam. Don't stand around in a circle with the other kids and talk about difficult questions. The neuroscientists I spoke with also advised exercise to recharge a tired brain.

You're probably not going to do jumping jacks in front of friends and strangers at a standardized test center, but walk up and down the hallways to get your body moving. Just don't stray too far.

Don't worry if you miss a string of questions.

A bad run won't kill your score. Keep positive and focused.

Push through fatigue.

There may be a time near the end of the test when you just can't think clearly. Push through it. Close your eyes for a moment and take two deep breaths. Like a runner, you'll get your second wind.

After the Test

What should I do?

Forget about the exam and go get something to eat.

Summary

If nothing else, remember the following three pieces of advice:

* Do some exercise on the morning of your test.
* Wear layered clothing and bring an extra sweatshirt.
* If you get tired, push through the fatigue.

CHAPTER 8

THE RESULTS

What to do

Basic Facts

How long until scores come out?

Your results will come within the following time periods:

*   SAT and SAT Subject Tests – Scores are available online 17-19 days after the exam.
*   ACT – Scores are available two and a half weeks after the exam.
*   PSAT – Scores are available in mid-December.
*   ISEE – Scores are available 7-10 days after the test. You can

sign up for expedited delivery, which will get you your scores on the first Monday, Wednesday or Friday after the exam.

* SSAT – Scores are available about 10 days after the exam.
* SHSAT – Scores are not released until March.

What's a good score?

It depends on the school you're trying to get into. Ask an admissions representative about the median score range.

What if I think they made a mistake scoring my test?

This is a tough sell. With the ISEE, you can request hand scoring, which will help if you made a mistake bubbling in the answer sheet. With most other tests, you're not going to have much luck.

If you're absolutely positive that something went wrong, keep calling the testing organization; eventually they may break.

How do I handle a bad score?

If it's the SAT, ACT, ISEE or SSAT, and you can take it again, sign up to take it again. If you took the SAT or ACT and ordered a copy of the test, go over what went wrong. If you didn't order a copy of the test, and it's available for your test date, order a copy and go over what went wrong.

If you took the PSAT, don't worry about it. But know that you should start preparing for the SAT or ACT earlier than you had originally planned.

If you took the ISEE and can't take it again, there may still be time to take the SSAT (and vice-versa). Many private schools and some boarding schools accept either test, so give it a shot.

If you took the SHSAT or one of the other tests for the final time, there's not much you can do.

In my experience, what someone did at school mattered much more than where they went. It may sound like a rotten consolation, but struggling is an important part of growth. It helps make you more understanding of other people so you don't end up being a gigantic jerk later in life.

Most importantly, understand that a bad test score doesn't mean failure in life. It's a test; it's not a final statement about your worth or ability to succeed in the future.

Do schools see all of my scores?

It depends on which test you took. Some high schools put your test scores on your transcript. If yours does, you can ask them not to.

* **SAT**

   Most colleges allow you to send only the test scores you want to send. However, some schools have different policies (Yale, for example, wants to see all of your SAT scores).

   The College Board has a policy called Score Choice, which lets you choose which scores are made available to colleges. I suggest not making your scores available. It gives you more control over who sees them. Again, some schools want to see all of your scores, and Score Choice won't override that demand. Do check.

* **ACT**

  The ACT works like the SAT, and you can choose which schools see your scores. The ACT also lets you completely delete a score, so no one can see it, which can be very helpful.

* **SSAT and ISEE**

  You can choose which schools see which scores.

If I bomb the first time I take a test but do well the second time, will my bad score hurt my chances of getting into school?

No. A testing company may look into it if your score goes up an insane amount (800 points on the SAT, for example), but they're not going to treat you like a criminal.

What do you mean, look into it?

They're not going to take blood samples. You'll be assumed innocent, so as long as you didn't cheat, don't worry about it.

If I do worse the second time, which score will schools count?

Admission counselors understand that students have bad days. They will take the higher score when considering a student's application.

I bombed my first test, and I'm taking it again; what should I do?

These tests can cause anxiety. Even with mock exams, some students need to get one bad score out of the way before they can test to their ability. That said, try to figure out what happened on the first test.

Answer the following questions honestly:

* Did you study as much as you could?
* Did you go over your weak areas?
* Did you believe you could do well?
* On the test, did you fight through the difficult questions?

If the answer to any of the above questions is no, you know what to change. Dedicate yourself to every part of the process this time around.

If there's another test coming up, take that test. You've built up momentum and put in a lot of hours. Waiting six months to take the test again wastes a lot of effort. The only exception is if you scored way below your intended score and need a lot more tutoring and time to improve.

A final note about colleges.

My most successful friend never finished college. He succeeded because he worked hard and never got discouraged. Another successful friend, who's now a college professor, bounced around a number of schools before getting his degree in his mid-twenties from USC.

Times have changed, and a degree from an Ivy league school isn't a guarantee of success, nor is a degree from a non-Ivy a harbinger of doom. School is school; it's what you do there and after you graduate that really counts.

Howard Gardner, Ph.D, a developmental psychologist and Harvard professor of education and cognition, is best known for his theory of multiple intelligences, which has changed the way people view what it means to be smart. He gives the best quote I've seen about our educational system:

> *The time has come to broaden our notion of the spectrum of talents. The single most important contribution education can make to a child's development is to help him toward a field where his talents best suit him, where he will be satisfied and competent. We've completely lost sight of that. Instead we subject everyone to an education where, if you succeed, you will be best suited to be a college professor. And we evaluate everyone along the way according to whether they meet that narrow standard of success. We should spend less time ranking children and more time helping them to identify their natural competencies and gifts, and cultivate those. There are hundreds and hundreds of ways to succeed, and many, many different abilities that will help you get there.*

Summary

If you did well on your exam, congratulations.

If you didn't do as well as you wanted, and you can take the exam again, start studying, but first evaluate what went wrong.

Ask yourself if you studied enough and studied your weaknesses. Did you take mock exams? If you didn't, start. If you did and you still scored poorly, write it off as a bad day and keep studying. Many students have one bad test before they score to their potential.

If you can't take the test again, accept what happened and learn from it. Struggle can be a very positive event in your life if you let it.

Most of all, remember that it's just a test. It's important, but it doesn't determine your life. Only you can do that.

APPENDIX

THE SAT

The SAT used to be the S.A.T., which stood for Scholastic Aptitude Test. It lost the right to this name when it was proven that it wasn't actually a test of aptitude. So the name was changed to the Scholastic Assessment Test, until it was proven that it wasn't an assessment either. After this second embarrassment, the S.A.T. just became the SAT. It stands for nothing, and that should tell you something.

Who takes it and why?

The SAT is taken by high school juniors and seniors for admission to college.

What's on it?

* Two math sections that test arithmetic, algebra and geometry
* One reading section that tests reading and data analysis
* One writing and language section that tests grammar and data analysis
* One "optional" essay

"Optional" is in quotes because for many students, the schools they want to attend require it, which makes it not so optional.

There may be a short, experimental section on your SAT, which can be either math, reading or grammar and does not count toward your score. The purpose of the section is to test questions for future exams.

All questions are multiple choice, except for 13 math questions for which students must supply the answers.

Can I use a calculator?

On one of the math sections, you can use a calculator. On the other, you can't. You will not be asked to do complicated arithmetic on the calculator-prohibited section, but you will have to do some multiplication and division.

How is it scored?

Your reading and your writing and language scores will be combined into an Evidence-Based Reading and Writing Score which ranges from 200 to 800. Your two math sections will also be combined for a score from 200 to 800, for a total range of 400–1600. The essay is scored across three sections: reading, writing and analysis, all of which range from 2-8 (two graders will give you a score of 1-4. These scores are combined).

The SAT allows super-scoring, which allows students to combine scores from different tests. So if you did better on math on the May exam, but better in Evidence-Based Reading and Writing on the October exam, you can combine your May math score with your October reading and grammar scores into one super score.

How long is It

The SAT has 4 or 5 sections, depending on whether you take the essay. Counting breaks, it lasts around four hours if you take the essay, three hours without it.

How many times can I take it?

You can take the SAT as many times as you want. College counselors recommend taking it at most three times. Any more and you may come across to colleges as obsessive.

What is Score Choice?

Score Choice allows you to control which schools see your test scores. Some people view Score Choice as freedom to take the SAT as many times as possible, but there are risks with this approach. First, some schools demand to see all your tests. While only a small number of schools currently have this requirement, a school can change its policy at any time.

In addition, the SAT is stressful and takes your focus away from school work. You're better served, in my opinion, by limiting the number of times you take the test.

Are past tests available?

Yes. Eight SAT exams are free online at

> https://collegereadiness.collegeboard.org/sat/
> practice/full-length-practice-tests.

The Official SAT Study Guide has the same eight exams compiled into a book.

When should I start studying?

Take a mock exam at the end of your sophomore year of high school. It'll show you how far you have to go and where you're strong and weak.

When should I take it?

The SAT is offered is August, October, November, December, March, May and June. During your junior year, take it at least once.

As for when, take it when your mock exam scores approach your target score. If you want a 1400 and you're scoring near that on your mock exams, you're ready.

Can I order a copy of the test?

If you take the March, May or October SAT, you can order the Question and Answer Service, which gets you a copy of your test, which specific questions you missed and the answer key. It's extremely valuable; get it.

Honestly, does this test suck?

Yeah, the SAT pretty much sucks. But all standardized tests suck at least a little bit. Your best way to stay sane and get better is to get the actual tests and practice with those questions.

Some misconceptions about the SAT

Juniors shouldn't take the exam until March or May

There's some basic trigonometry on the exam, and the algebra is complicated, but if you're in an advanced math class, you can handle it. If you're scoring high on your mock exams at the end of October, you're ready to take it in November.

Certain months have easier/harder tests than others

Not true. Certain tests are harder than others, but there's no correlation between the month a test is given and its difficulty.

Certain months have easier curves than others

Again, not true. The College Board creates a curve for the entire year.

THE ACT

The ACT is an alternative to the SAT. It started in the Midwest but has been gaining traction lately on the coasts as college admissions have gotten more competitive.

Who takes it and why?

The ACT is taken by high school juniors and seniors for admission to college.

What's on it?

There is one section of each of the following topics:

* English, which tests grammar and style
* Math, which covers arithmetic up to basic trigonometry
* Reading comprehension
* Science[+]
* An optional essay

[+]You generally don't need to know specific scientific facts, such as the periodic table or physics formulas. You will be given results or tables from scientific experiments and asked questions about them. One or two questions may require outside scientific knowledge, but it will be basic knowledge.

All questions are multiple choice.

Are calculators allowed?

Yes.

How is it scored?

Each section (except the essay) is scored from 1-36. If you do the essay, it's scored from 2-12 and not factored into your overall score.

The ACT allows super-scoring, which allows students to combine scores from different tests. So if you did better on math on the April exam, but better in reading on the June exam, you can combine your April math score with your June reading score into one super score.

How long is it?

If you do the essay, the ACT lasts around four hours. Without the essay it's around three and a half hours.

How many times can I take it?

Take the ACT as many times as you want. You can completely delete your score, so no one will ever know. That said, The ACT is stressful and takes focus away from school work.

Are past tests available?

Yes, many ACT tests have been released; however, the ACT has changed recently in that the math and science sections have gotten harder and the essay has changed its focus. *The Real ACT Prep Guide* has three of the new exams. *The ACT Prep Pack* contains the book along with two extra online exams and a slew of extra questions. Get the Prep Pack.

Older exams are still helpful, but may not be accurate predictors of your math and science scores.

When should I start studying?

Take a mock exam at the end of your sophomore year of high school. You'll see how far you have to go and where you're strong and weak.

When should I take the ACT?

The ACT is offered in September, October, December, February, April and June. You should take it when your mock exam scores are within your target range.

Honestly, does this test suck?

Yes, it does. ACT questions are more like school question than SAT questions are, but the ACT is a test of speed. If you're not a fast worker, this test may not be for you.

SHOULD I TAKE THE SAT OR THE ACT?

There's a lot of advice about whether to take the SAT or ACT and most of it is misleading. There are many similarities between the two exams, but each test has aspects that make it better suited for certain students and worse for others. Here are the basics:

Take the SAT if:

The SAT favors students who can handle uncertainty and work through questions that seem complicated at first read. Students who should take the SAT can apply their knowledge to new question types, as SAT problems force students to be flexible with their knowledge, especially in math and grammar.

In addition, math counts for half of your SAT score but only a quarter of your ACT score. So if you're great at math, and not so great at reading and grammar, the SAT is for you.

Take the ACT if:

The ACT favors students who work quickly, read well and are not science-phobic. ACT questions are closer to regular schoolwork and are, in my opinion, fairer than SAT questions. That said, the ACT is about speed. If you're not a fast worker, especially a fast reader, the ACT will be a challenge.

Take a full test of each and compare your scores.

There are other differences between the two exams – but it's difficult to tell how these differences will affect a particular student.

Avoid mini-exams that give you 10-20 questions from each test. These mini-exams don't account for speed or stamina: it's like walking a mile to see how you'll do on a marathon.

The best way to tell which test is better for you is to take a *full* mock exam in both. Take an actual test, not one created by a test prep company. Then compare your scores. There are SAT/ACT score conversion charts on the internet. A good one is https://blog.prepscholar.com/act-to-sat-conversion.

Schools don't value one test over the other. If a school accepts both the ACT and SAT, then it values both tests equally.

THE PSAT

PSAT stands for Preliminary SAT. It's also called PSAT/ NMSQT. The latter acronym stands for National Merit Scholarship Qualifying Test. The PSAT is made by the people who make the SAT, so its question types and methodology are the same as those on the SAT.

Who takes it and why?

Students take the PSAT in October of their junior year to qualify for National Merit Scholarships. A link for more information on National Merit Scholarships appears later in this chapter. Sophomores can take a practice PSAT, called the PPSAT, but their scores won't count for merit scholarships.

Will a bad score hurt my chances of getting into a good college?

No, colleges don't care. Winning a National Merit Scholarship looks great on an application, but not winning one won't hurt you.

What's on it?

* Two math sections that test basic arithmetic, algebra and geometry
* One critical reading section that tests reading and data analysis
* One grammar section that tests grammar and data analysis

All questions are multiple choice, except for 10 math questions for which you must supply the answers.

Are calculators allowed?

On one of the math sections, you can use a calculator. On the other, you can't. You will not be asked to do complicated arithmetic on the calculator-prohibited section, but you will have to do some multiplication and division.

How is it scored?

Your reading and your writing and language scores will be combined into an Evidence-Based Reading and Writing Score which ranges from 160 to 760. Your two math sections will also be combined for a score from 160 to 760, for a total range of 320–1520.

How long is it?

The PSAT has four sections and lasts a little over two hours.

When should I start studying?

Take a mock exam at the end of your sophomore year of high school. You'll see how far you have to go and where you're strong and weak.

Honestly, does this test suck?

It sucks a little, but because it doesn't affect you much it's not a big deal. Every standardized test sucks a little, and the PSAT is a good way to tell how much work you need to do before taking the SAT.

SAT SUBJECT TESTS

A long time ago, the SAT Subject Tests were called the Achievement Tests. Then they were called SAT IIs. They are single-subject exams that last an hour. There are Subject Tests for almost every subject, from Chinese to U.S. history to physics.

Who takes them and why?

SAT Subject Tests can be taken by high school students of any year. Students take them because some colleges require them. Many colleges want none; some colleges want two, and a small number want three. Check to be sure.

If you're applying to be an engineer, you should take the Math Level 2 Subject Test, as well as either Chemistry or Physics.

Are calculators allowed?

You can use a calculator for the math exams, but NOT for physics or chemistry.

How are they scored?

Each test is scored from 200 to 800.

How many questions are on each exam?

Depending on the subject, there will be between 50 and 90 questions. All are multiple choice.

Can I take the SAT Subject Test for a language I grew up speaking?

Yes. If you grew up speaking Spanish, for example, you can take the Spanish SAT Subject Test. I don't think colleges will be impressed by a high score, however.

Are past tests available?

The Official Study Guide for all SAT Subject Tests has an actual exam for each SAT Subject Test offered. It's an invaluable resource. Get it.

When should I take them?

The best time to take an SAT Subject Test is in June of the year you took that class. So if you're a sophomore and taking biology, take the Biology Subject Test in June of your sophomore year.

Honestly, do they suck?

Meh. They're somewhat irritating, but they don't suck as badly as the actual SAT or ACT. You'll need to study, though.

THE ISEE

ISEE stands for Independent School Entrance Exam. It's given by the Educational Records Bureau. The Educational Records Bureau also administers a test called the ERB, which many private school students take at the end of each year. The ISEE and the ERB are different tests, and doing well on the ERB does not mean you'll necessarily do well on the ISEE.

Who takes it and why?

The ISEE is for admission to private schools. There are four different ISEE exams: Primary, Lower, Middle and Upper Level. Which test you take is determined by your grade:

The ISEE Primary is for students currently in first, second and third grades.

The Lower Level ISEE is for students currently in fourth and fifth grades.

The Middle Level ISEE is for students currently in sixth and seventh grades.

The Upper Level ISEE is for students currently in eighth, ninth and 10th grades.

What's on it?

The ISEE Primary has reading and math.

The Lower, Middle and Upper Level ISEE have:

* A verbal section that tests vocabulary in the form of synonyms and sentence completions
* Two different math sections
* A reading comprehension section
* An optional essay

All questions are multiple choice.

Are calculators allowed?

Nope.

How is it scored?

There will be three scores on your ISEE report: a scaled score, a percentile rank, and a stanine score. Don't worry about the scaled score. The percentile rank tells you how you did versus your peers: an 85 percent on a given section means you scored better than 85 percent of all the other students in your grade who took the test over the last three years. The percentile rank is translated into a stanine score that ranges from 1-9. It's the stanine score that schools care about.

The essay is not scored. Schools may look at this essay, however, so make sure you try your best.

Within each section are five or six experimental questions that aren't counted towards a student's score. The ERB is testing these questions for future exams. It's impossible to tell which questions are experimental, so students should try their hardest on each question.

How long is it?

* The ISEE Primary is around an hour and a half.
* The Lower Level ISEE is around two and a half hours.
* The Middle and Upper Level ISEE are around three hours.

How many times can I take it?

Students can take the ISEE once per cycle. The cycles are August- November, December-March and April-July.

Are past tests available?

One actual ISEE exam has been released by the ERB and is available on their website. Details are listed later in the Appendix.

The Upper Level ISEE is for eighth-to-10th graders, so if you're in eighth grade, don't expect to answer every question correctly. The second math section of the released ISEE has some very difficult problems, including a trigonometry question. (If you don't know what trigonometry is, it's math that students normally learn in 11th grade.) Don't judge your score by your percentage, as you would a normal math test at school. Instead, look at what you missed and figure out what you need to learn.

When should I take the ISEE?

If you're applying for regular admission to private school, you should sign up for the November and December tests.

When should I start studying?

Take a mock exam in March of the calendar year you'll take the exam. You'll learn how far you have to go and where you're strong and weak. A common mistake students make is waiting until September to start prepping for the ISEE. Vocabulary and reading, which are both difficult to improve quickly, account for 50% of your grade on this exam. Find out before the summer how much time you need to prepare.

Honestly, does this test suck?

Yup. The ISEE is pretty sucky. The alternative, the SSAT, is even worse, though, so you're stuck with it.

THE SSAT

SSAT stands for Secondary School Admission Test and is created by The Enrollment Management Association.

Who takes it and why?

The SSAT is for admission to boarding schools and some private high schools. There is an Elementary Level, a Lower Level and an Upper Level SSAT. Which test you take is determined by grade:

The Elementary Level SSAT is for students currently in third and fourth grades.

The Lower Level SSAT is for students currently in fifth, sixth and seventh grades.

The Upper Level SSAT is for students currently in eighth, ninth, 10th and 11th grades.

What's on it?

* A verbal section that tests vocabulary in the form of synonyms and analogies
* Two different math sections
* A reading comprehension section
* An optional essay

All questions are multiple choice.

Are calculators allowed?

Nope.

How is it scored?

An SSAT score report has a score, a range, a percentile for your gender and a percentile for your total grade. The percentile, which measures you against your peers, is all that matters. An 85 percent on a given section means you scored better than 85 percent of all the other students in your grade who took the test over the last three years It is the percentages for your total grade that schools care about.

The essay is not scored. Schools may look at this essay, however, so make sure you try your best.

How long is it?

* The Elementary Level SSAT is a little over two hours.
* The Lower and Upper Levels are a little under three hours.

How many times can I take it?

You can take the SSAT as often as you like, but know that studying for it is time-consuming and takes away from school work.

Definitely take it more than once. The tests differ wildly in terms of difficulty. One year, I had students say the math on the November test was impossible and the December test math was much easier. The next year it was reversed.

Are past tests available?

Two Middle and Upper Level SSAT exams are available in a book you can order at ssat.org. I've found that the math on the Upper Level SSAT exams is not an accurate representation of the math on the actual SSAT. Too many students have come back from the actual exam and said the math was much harder than it was on the practice exams.

For the Elementary Level SSAT, a free, half-length practice test for each grade can be downloaded at ssat.org.

When is the test offered?

The SSAT is offered every month from October through April, and again in June. It is not offered in May or from July through September.

When should I take the SSAT?

I've found the best time for students to take the SSAT is in November and December.

When should I start studying?

Take a mock exam around March of the calendar year you'll take the exam. How you do will let you know how far you have to go and where you're strong and weak.

A common mistake students make is waiting until September to start prepping for the SSAT. Vocabulary and reading, which are both difficult to improve quickly, account for two-thirds of your score. Find out early how much time you need to prepare.

Honestly, does this test suck?

Yup. The SSAT sucks. Check to see if the school you're applying to also accepts the ISEE, which is a slightly better test (but still sucks).

THE SHSAT

The SHSAT, or Specialized High School Admission Test, is the best of the standardized tests. It's timed, but in a way that allows for more flexibility and freedom than other exams. It doesn't test vocabulary, and it has more interesting questions.

Who takes it and why?

The SHSAT is used for admission to test-in public high schools, such as Stuyvesant and Bronx Science in New York City. Your admission is completely dependent on your score.

You can take the SHSAT as an 8th or 9th grader. The tests are different only in the difficulty of the questions.

What's on it?

The SHSAT has a math and a English language arts section. The ELA section contains:

* Grammar, syntax and editing
* Reading comprehension

The math section contains:

* Math questions

There are 114 questions, 57 in each section, but only 47 in each section are scored. The remaining 20 questions are experimental and are being tested for future exams.

There are five math questions for which you'll have to enter your own answers. The rest are multiple choice.

Are calculators allowed?

Nope.

How is it scored?

The number of questions you get right is converted to a scaled score between 32 and 800. The cutoff score for top schools varies each year, but it's usually around 560.

You're scored only against the people in your grade

How long is it?

The SHSAT is three hours. Unlike other standardized tests, there aren't individually timed sections on the SHSAT. You can divide your time as you need to, and you can jump back and forth between sections.

How many times can I take it?

Students can take the SHSAT once a year.

Are past tests available?

The SHSAT changed in 2017, so while there are a couple practice exams available online, as of publication, these aren't actual past tests.

Definitely practice with the available practice tests to get a sense of the types of questions you'll see.

When is the test offered?

The SHSAT is offered in late October or early November.

When should I start studying?

Take a mock exam around February. How you do will show you how far you have to go and where you're strong and weak.

A common mistake students make is waiting until September to start prepping for the SHSAT. The test is difficult, and getting into a top school is competitive. Start early; definitely take a mock exam before the summer.

Honestly, does this test suck?

No. The SHSAT is about as fair as it gets when it comes to standardized tests. You may not love it, but you could do much worse.

CANCELING YOUR SCORES

You can cancel your scores on the ACT, SAT and SAT Subject Tests, but only before you see your scores. It's tough to say whether you should, and it depends on you. Do you consistently think you bombed school exams, only to get them back with high grades, or do you usually know when you have done poorly on an exam? Exactly what makes you think you bombed the exam?

Remember that with most schools, you have control over which test scores they see. So if you know you're not applying to a school that requires every score, a bad test doesn't matter.

Canceling an SAT score

Students have two options for canceling their scores:

* You can fill out a form at the test center before you leave. You'll get this form from your proctor.
* You can fill out a cancellation form and mail or fax it to the College Board offices.

If you choose the second option, here's the link to the cancellation form:

http://sat.collegeboard.org/scores/cancel-sat-scores

You have until midnight on the Wednesday following the exam, and you cannot cancel by phone or email. You cannot cancel your SAT scores after you've seen them.

Canceling SAT Subject Test scores

You can cancel your scores during the test; you just need to ask the proctor. Or you can do so online no later than 11:59pm EST on the Thursday after the test. The link to cancel is:

collegereadiness.collegeboard.org/sat-subject-tests/scores/canceling-scores

Know that if you took multiple Subject Tests, you must cancel *all* of your scores for that day. If you cancel one, you cancel them all. The only exception is if your calculator breaks on the Math Level 1 or Level 2 exam. If that happens, you must:

* Report the equipment failure during the test.
* Fill out and sign a Request to Cancel Test Scores form, checking off "Single Subject Test Equipment Failure."
* Return the completed form to the room supervisor before leaving.

You cannot cancel your math Subject Test score due to equipment failure after you've left the test center.

How do I delete an ACT score?

You must send a written request with your name and home address to:

ACT Institutional Services
PO Box 168
Iowa City, IA 52243-0168

The ACT will send you the proper form.

Obviously, don't delete an ACT score until you have a higher ACT score on record.

Be aware: you cannot delete a test score that's already been sent to colleges! To avoid this ever happening, do the following: When you sign up to take the ACT, the registration form will ask for the schools you want to see your results. Leave this blank and request that your scores not be made available to colleges or to your high school.

TEST REGISTRATION

SAT and SAT Subject Tests

To register — sat.collegeboard.org/register
Questions via email — collegeboard.org/contact-us/
send-message/
(212) 713-8000

ACT

To register — actstudent.org/regist/index.html
Questions — (319) 337-1270

ISEE

To register — iseeonline.erblearn.org
Questions via email — isee_online@erblearn.org
(800) 446-0320

SSAT

To register — www.ssat.org
Questions via email — info@sssat.org
(609) 683-4440

SHSAT

You must register through your guidance counselor.

PSAT

Your school takes care of registration.

WHERE TO FIND THE ACTUAL TESTS

SAT

The Official SAT Study Guide is available at most bookstores and online. It contains 8 SAT exams with real SAT questions. You can also download the tests for free on the College Board website.

There's also an online course run by the College Board, and many practice problems on Khan Academy.

SAT Subject Tests

The Official Study Guide for all SAT Subject Tests is available on-line and at some bookstores. True to its name, it contains one practice test for every SAT Subject Test offered.

ACT

The Official ACT Prep Guide has three actual ACT exams. It also has detailed answers and explanations of why each right answer is right AND why every wrong answer is wrong. The ACT is extremely consistent, so this book is invaluable.

The Official ACT Prep Pack has everything in the *The Official ACT Prep Guide*, plus a mobile app, extra questions and two extra online tests. Get the Prep Pack. It's available online and at some bookstores.

ISEE

What to Expect on the ISEE is available for the Lower, Middle and Upper Level exams. You can download it for free at:

http://isee.erblearn.org/guide.aspx

The webpage listed also has some practice problems and a long explanation of what to expect on the ISEE. There's a column that runs down the left of the page. At the top of the column is the prompt "Select Level." Use this to select the right level test.

The ISEE Primary is for students currently in first, second and third grades.

The Lower Level ISEE is for students currently in fourth and fifth grades.

The Middle Level ISEE is for students currently in sixth and seventh grades.

The Upper Level ISEE is for students currently in eighth, ninth and 10th grades.

Most students are absolutely destroyed by this practice test, and the experience will help put into perspective just how much studying you need. Get these exams.

The mobile app Milestone Math is extremely helpful for preparing students for the math sections of this exam. I created it, so I know.

SSAT

Two versions of both the Lower and Upper Level SSAT are available in a booklet you can order for $30 here:

http://www.ssat.org/ssat/test/test-prep-orderguide.html

As I said previously, students have said that the math on the actual exam was harder than the math on these practice tests.

The Elementary Level SSAT is for students currently in third and fourth grades.

The Lower Level SSAT is for students currently in fifth, sixth and seventh grades.

The Upper Level SSAT is for students currently in eighth, ninth, 10th and 11th grades.

The mobile app Milestone Math is extremely helpful for preparing students for the math sections of this exam. I created it, so I know.

SHSAT

You can access two practice SHSAT exams when you download the SHSAT handbook from the Department of Education website:

schools.nyc.gov/NR/rdonlyres/ 39E5EC65-FA08-4A2A-91AD-9F7334670B3D/0/20172018SpecializedHighSchoolsStudentHandbookENGLISH.pdf

Or just Google "released SHSAT tests," and the above link should be the first result.

The mobile app Milestone Math is extremely helpful for preparing students for the math section of this exam. I created it, so I know.

READING AND VIEWING RECOMMENDATIONS

Dealing with Stress
youtube.com/watch?v=YmxBBo-sxUE
The Anti-Anxiety Toolkit — Melissa Tiers

Emotional Control and Intelligence
Mindset — Carol Dweck*

*This book contains one very important point, made over and over again. It's worth getting, but once you get the point you can stop reading.

Changing Habits
Switch — Chip and Dan Heath
59 Seconds — Richard Wiseman

General Happiness
The Happiness Hypothesis — Jonathan Haidt

Praising (or not) Your Child
Dweck, Carol. "The Perils and Promises of Praise."— *Educational Leadership* v65, n2 p34-39 Oct. 2007
NurtureShock — Po Bronson and Ashley Merryman

How the Brain Works
Brain Rules — John Medina

Anxiety and Performance
Choke — Sian Beilock

EXERCISES TO SHIFT YOUR FOCUS

Each morning, write down three things you're grateful for. Each night, write down five things that went right that day.

Do the above exercises for two weeks, and slowly your focus will shift to noticing and appreciating the good. What you're grateful for and what went right doesn't have to change every day: you can have repeats, but try to vary it when you can.

Breathing Exercises

Breathe in for a count of six.
Hold for a count of four.
Release for a count of eight.
Repeat for five breaths.

Meditation Exercises

Find a comfortable seated position. It can be on the floor or in a chair.

Set a timer for 10 minutes.

Close your eyes and concentrate on your breath. Don't try to control your breath; just let it come naturally.

When thoughts come, let them go and refocus on your breath. Some days you may be able to concentrate for long periods of time. Other days you might not get through three breaths before you lose focus. There is no good or bad meditation: it's all helpful.

ABOUT THE AUTHOR

Elie Venezky has been preparing students for standardized tests for more than 20 years. He has appeared on CNN, NPR and ABC. His former tutoring company, which he cofounded and at which he served as Educational Director, was voted in 2016 as one of the top 20 math tutoring companies in NYC out of over 2,000 companies assessed.

When he's not tutoring, Elie is an aerialist. He has performed trapeze, lyra and aerial dance in Europe and across the United States.

He lives in Brooklyn.

You know how to succeed on standardized tests.
Now get your parents the help they need.

Test Prep Sanity for Parents
*How to help your child excel on standardized tests
without driving each other crazy*

Made in United States
North Haven, CT
03 July 2022

20925042R00078